# Fun Facts about Hydrogen Chemistry for Kids

## The Element Series

## Children's Chemistry Books

As the simplest atom composed of one single proton contained in the nucleus being orbited by one electron, Hydrogen is the lightest and most element in our universe. It is the first element listed in the periodic table of elements. In this book, you will be learning about Hydrogen and how it is found and used in everyday life.

# Characteristics and Properties of Hydrogen

Hydrogen stems from Greek words "genes" (meaning creator), and "hydro" (meaning water). Antoine Lavoisier, a chemist from France named it.

1
H
Hydrogen
1.00794

HYDROGEN
STACJA TANKOWANIA WODORU

Hydrogen is an odorless, tasteless, and colorless gas at standard temperature. When it contacts oxygen, it will burn and since it is highly flammable it will burn with a flame that you cannot see.

Water, also known as H20, results when it is mixed with oxygen. Our bodies need water to survive. Have you had your eight glasses of water today?

Abstract
background with
molecules of water

$H^2$

Its gas consists of diatomic molecules called H2. Diatomic molecules consist of molecules composed of two atoms, which can be the same or different elements. The prefix di- is Greek, and means "two". When a diatomic molecule contains two atoms of the same element, such as oxygen (O2) or hydrogen (H2) it is then considered homonuclear.

Hydrogen has the symbol of H and the atomic number 1. Its weight is 1.00794 and is classified as a nonmetal phase when at room temperature. Its density is 0.08988 g/L @ 0 degrees Celsius. It melts at -259.14 degrees Celsius or -434.45 degrees Fahrenheit and boils at -252.87 degrees Celsius or -423.17 Fahrenheit. Since it can exist as a liquid under high pressure and at a very low temperature it is often stored in its liquid form so that it takes up less space than when it is in its regular gas form.

| 1 | 2 |
| --- | --- |
| **Hydrogen** | **Helium** |
| **H** | **He** |
| 1.00794 | 4.0026 |

| 3 |
| --- |
| **Lithium** |
| **Li** |
| 6.941 |

| 6 | 5 | 4 |
| --- | --- | --- |
| **Carbon** | **Boron** | **Beryllium** |
| **C** | **B** | **Be** |
| 12.0107 | 10.811 | 9.0122 |

# Where is it found on earth?

It is mostly found in water and each H20 molecule consists of two of its atoms. Hydrocarbons, hydroxides, and acids are just a few of the many compounds on our earth that are made with it.

H₂O

Proval Lake in
Pyatigorsk, Russia

Since it is very light, there is not much free hydrogen in our air because eventually it leaves and goes into space. On earth, it will only be found in its free form very deep into the underground.

# Stars and Planets

It is mostly found in gas planets and stars and the sun consists mostly of it, and plays a major role in providing power for the stars with fusion reactions. Since the pressure is very high far inside stars, its atoms convert to helium atoms. This process is known as fusion and when it releases the energy with heat this results in the sunlight we observe. Think about that the next time you are outside in the sun.

Blue hot sun

Anhydrous Ammonia

# How is hydrogen used today?

It is a very useful element being used to make refined metals, ammonia used for fertilizers, and methanol which is used to make artificial material including plastics.

It is also used commonly in petroleum and chemical industries as well as for a lot of physics and engineering applications, including welding or as a coolant.

High pressure
hydrogen tanks in
the car chassis.

A chemical factory with huge tanks and pipes

Have you seen rocket ships take off? They can do this because liquid hydrogen mixed with liquid oxygen creates a powerful explosion which is used a rocket fuel. NASA has developed a new human launch system which is designed to replace the space shuttle. For its first stage it uses solid propellants, for its second stage it uses liquid hydrogen and oxygen, and the service module uses liquid propellants so that it can reach the International Space Station.

A chemical compound with a molecular formula H2O2 is known to us as hydrogen peroxide. This is often used as a hair bleach or a cleaner. It is also possible, when mixed at certain concentrations, to use it to clean minor wounds. Think about this the next time you get a scrape on your knee. Your mom will probably grab that bottle of hydrogen peroxide and a bandage and then you are good to go!

HYDROGEN
PEROXIDE
16 FL OZ
(1 PT) 473 ml

HYDROGEN
FUEL CELL
Compressed
Hydrogen

To protect and keep our atmosphere clean, there is hope that one day it can be used as a cleaner fuel choice rather than fossil fuel. Car manufacturers are working with engineers to research the possible use of hydrogen gas as a viable and efficient fuel for cars and trucks. One possibility involves storing it in its solid state in car gas tanks. While there may be a lot of challenges involved, it might allow for more of its storage in vehicles, which means they can travel for a longer time period before stopping to refuel.

# How was it discovered?

In 1766, it was discovered by Henry Cavendish, a scientist from England. He experimented using hydrochloric acid and zinc and the result was hydrogen. It was at this same time that he discovered that when it burned it produced water. Scientists had produced it earlier, but were not aware of it as a unique element.

Henry
Cavendish

Nuclear sigh

# Ions and Isotopes

An ion is the result of molecule or atom containing a negative or positive charge since its electrons are not the same as the protons.

It becomes charged when the number of protons does not equal the number of electrons in the molecule or atom. The atom can have a negative charge or a positive charge contingent upon whether the electrons in the atom are greater than or less then its protons.

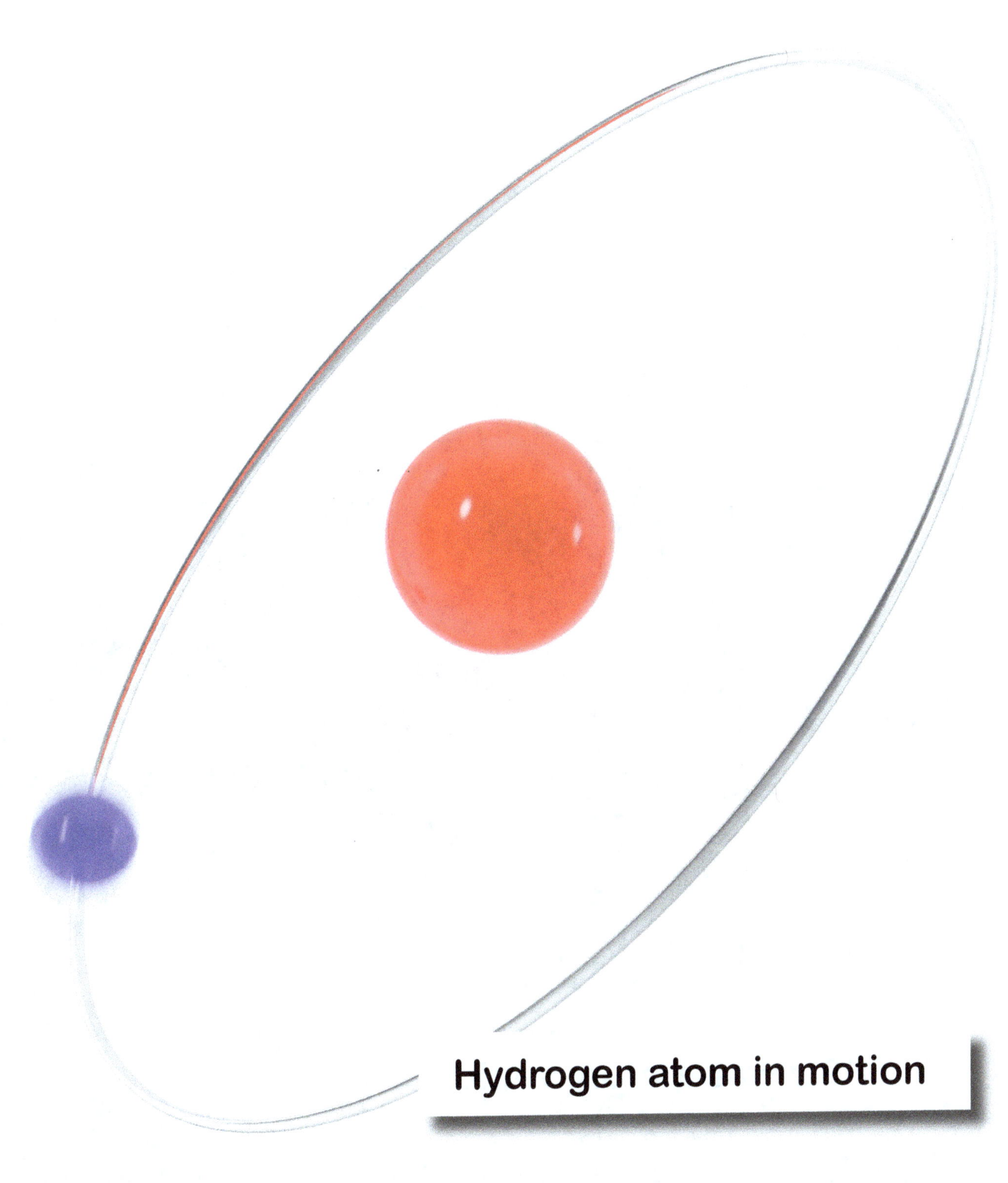


Hydrogen atom in motion

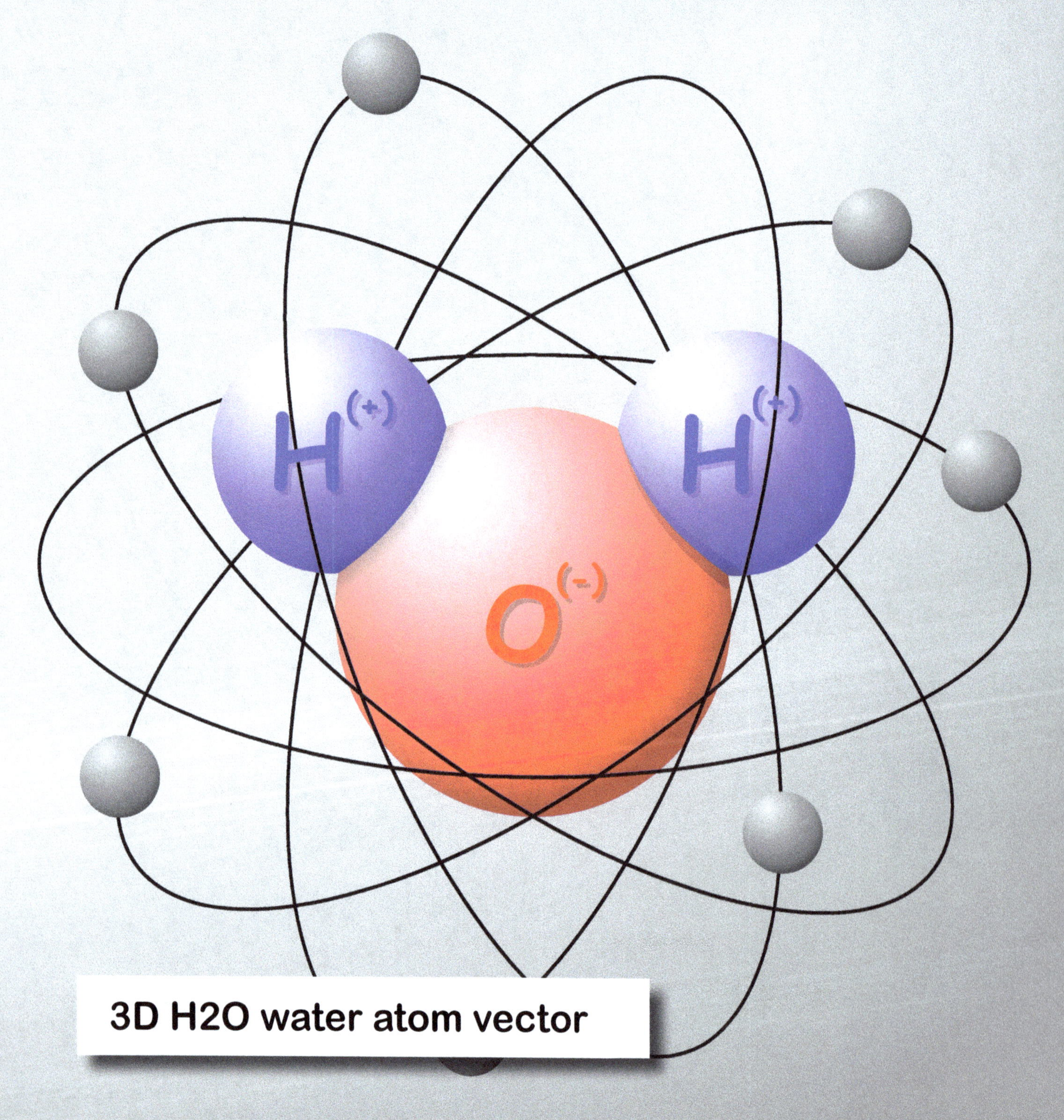


3D H2O water atom vector

Once an atom attaches to another atom due to its unequal number of proton and electrons, it becomes an ion.  An anion, (negative ion), contains more protons and less electrons.

An isotope is an atom that has the same number of electrons and protons, but the number of neutrons differs. When you change the number of neutrons, the element does not change. Element atoms with varying numbers of neutrons are named isotopes of that element.

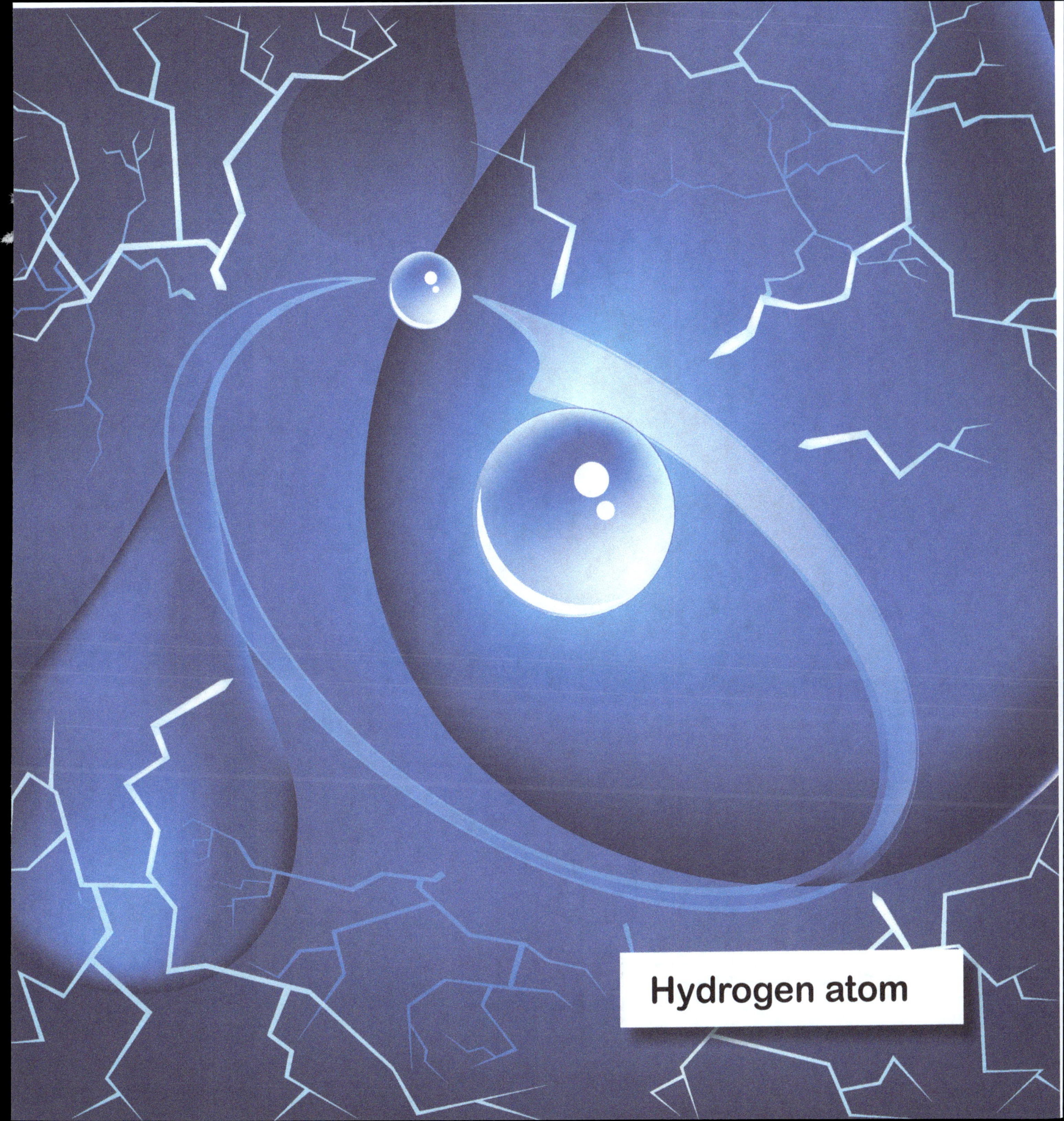
Hydrogen atom

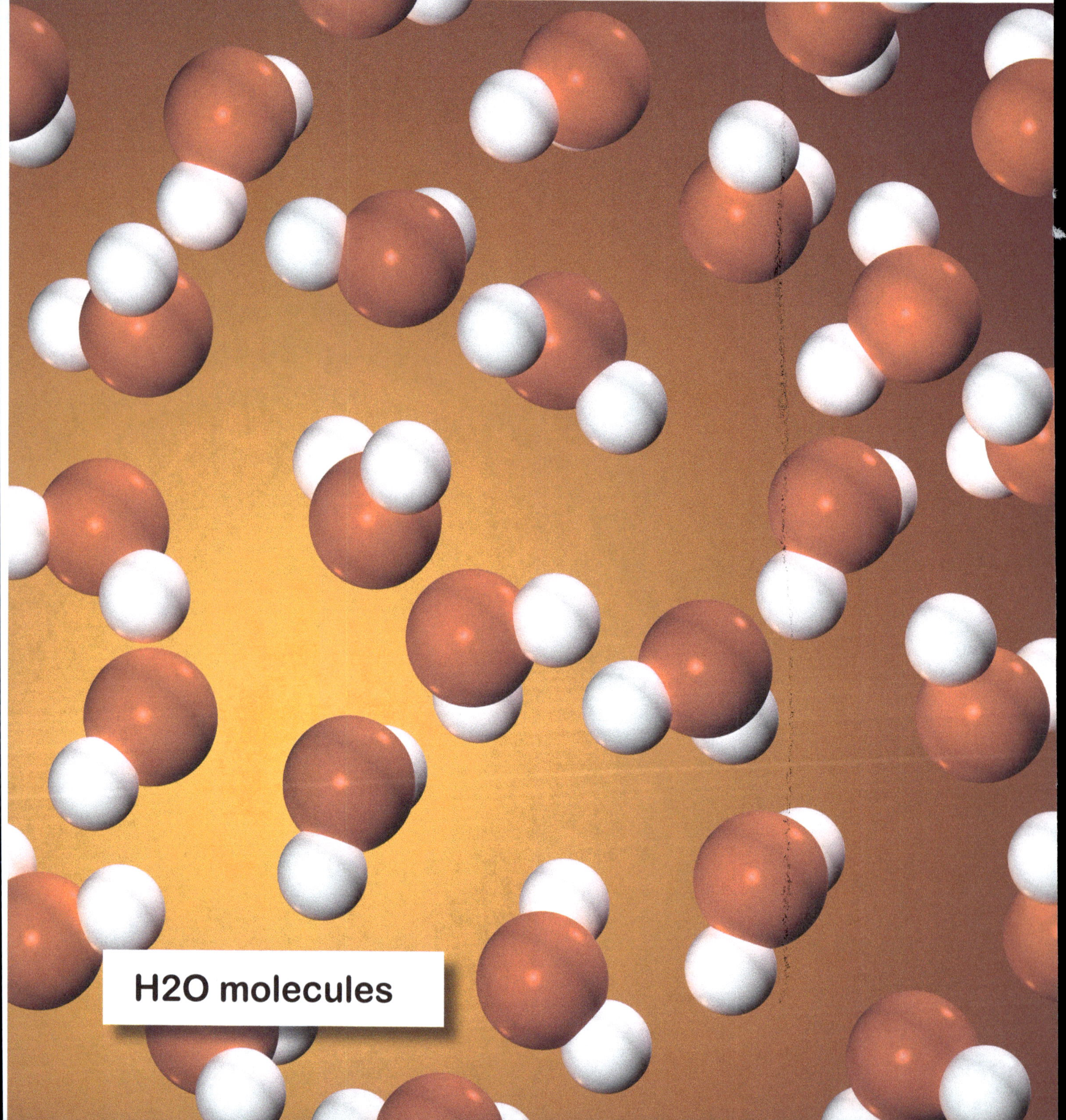
H2O molecules

When hydrogen takes on a charge that is negative it becomes an anion which is referred to as a hydride. A cation results when it takes on a positive charge. Its most common isotope is known as Protium. It contains no neutrons and only one proton. Deuterium and tritium are its other common isotopes.

# Interesting Facts about Hydrogen

It is estimated that it makes up more than 90 percent of all atoms contained in our universe and is the one element that exists without any neutrons. At high pressure and very low temperatures, it results in a liquid and under very high pressure it becomes liquid metal.

H2O molecule

Jupiter on Star Field

Jupiter, being a gas giant planet , may have metallic hydrogen in its core, as well as the other gas giant plants of the universe. It makes its transition to the metallic state under extreme compression. Scientists are researching this area to continue producing metallic hydrogen at a lower temperature and with static compression.

The human body consists of approximately 10 percent hydrogen. You will not be able to see this if you look at your body, but hydrogen as well as other elements are what makes the human body the miracle that it is.

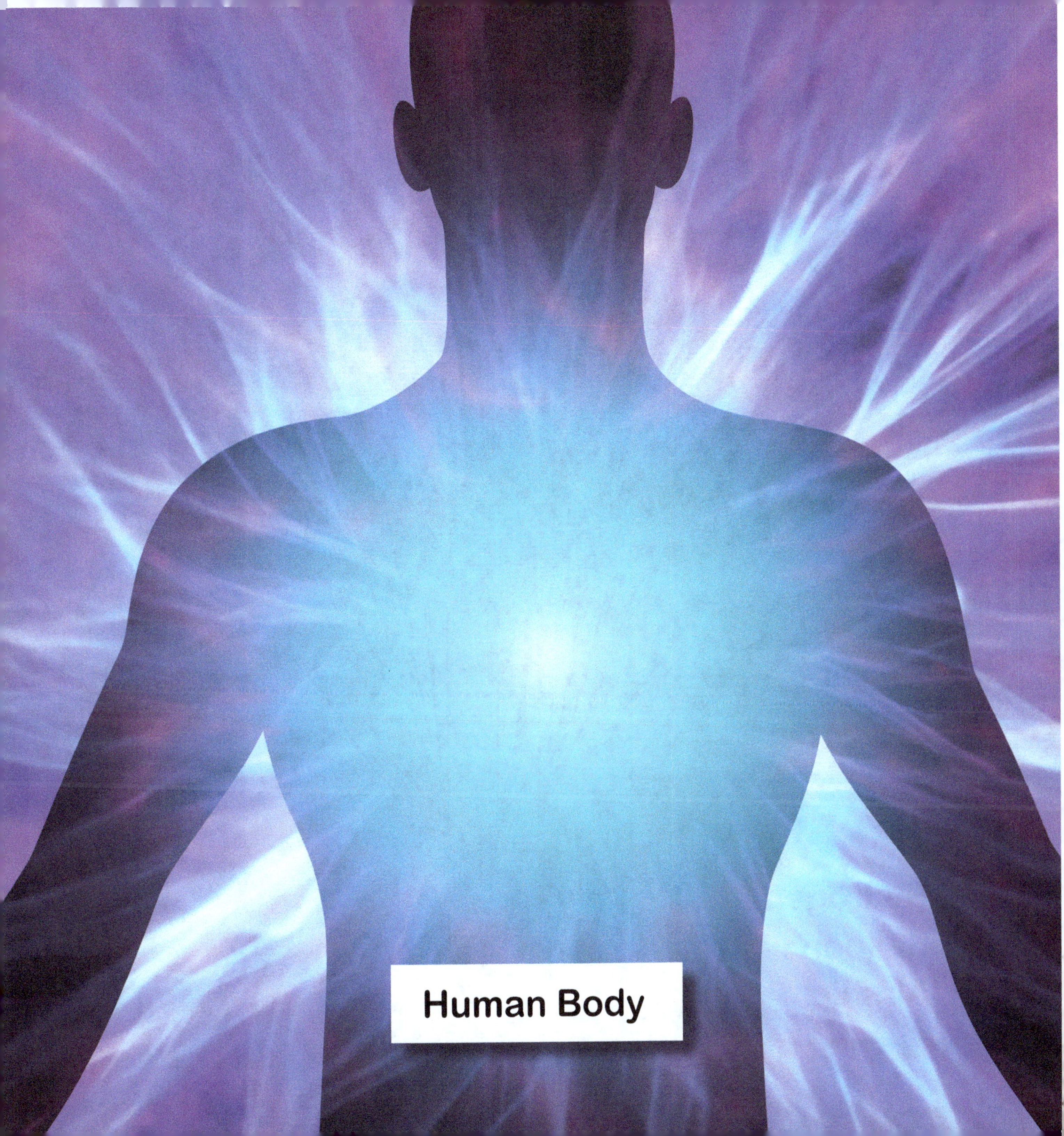

Human Body

Hydrogen
Balloon
Airship

Henri Giffard created the first lifted airship fueled by hydrogen. Airships later used it for airships called Zeppelins . They seemed to be reliable and safe most of the time, but after the Hindenburg disaster in 1937, they stopped using them. The Hindenburg was destroyed when a fire occurred midair above New Jersey and was broadcast live on the radio as well as being filmed.

Since it is very light, it has been utilized for lighter-than-air-balloons, but due to its flammable nature it became too dangerous.

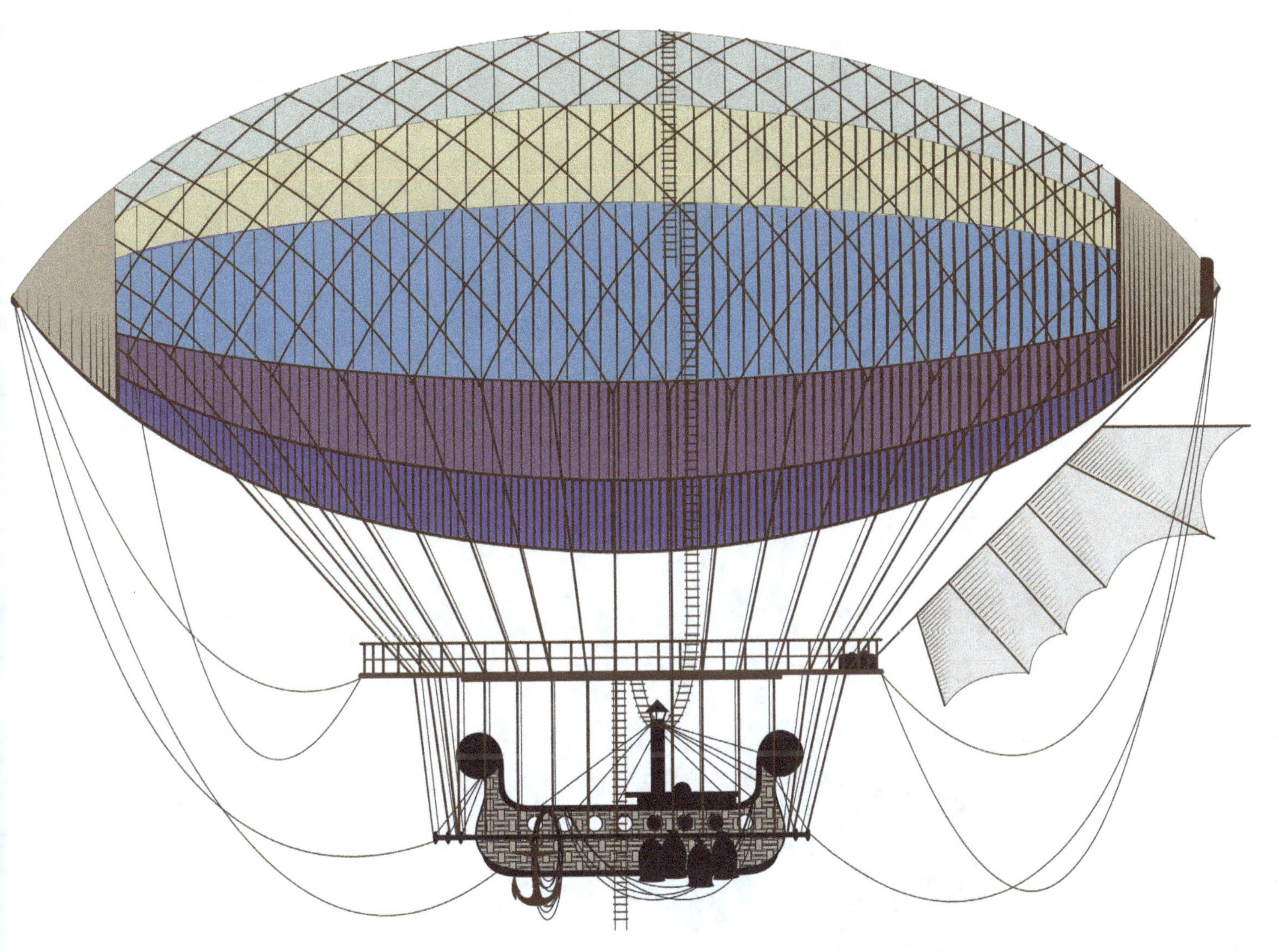

HYDROGEN
FLAMMABLE GAS
NO SMOKING
NO OPEN FLAME

Its gas can be created in a lab by combining dilute acid with metal. Please do not try this at home. It becomes dangerous to us as humans since fires may start when mixed with air, we are not able to breath it in its pure oxygen form, and it is also quite dangerous in the very cold liquid form.

# Periodic Table of Elements

There is so much more to learn about this element as well as the many other elements. You may want to research the periodic table of elements which lists all the elements including their atomic structure. In 1869, a Russian chemist named Dmitri Mendeleev came up with this table. With the use of this table, he had the ability to predict properties of elements prior to them being discovered.

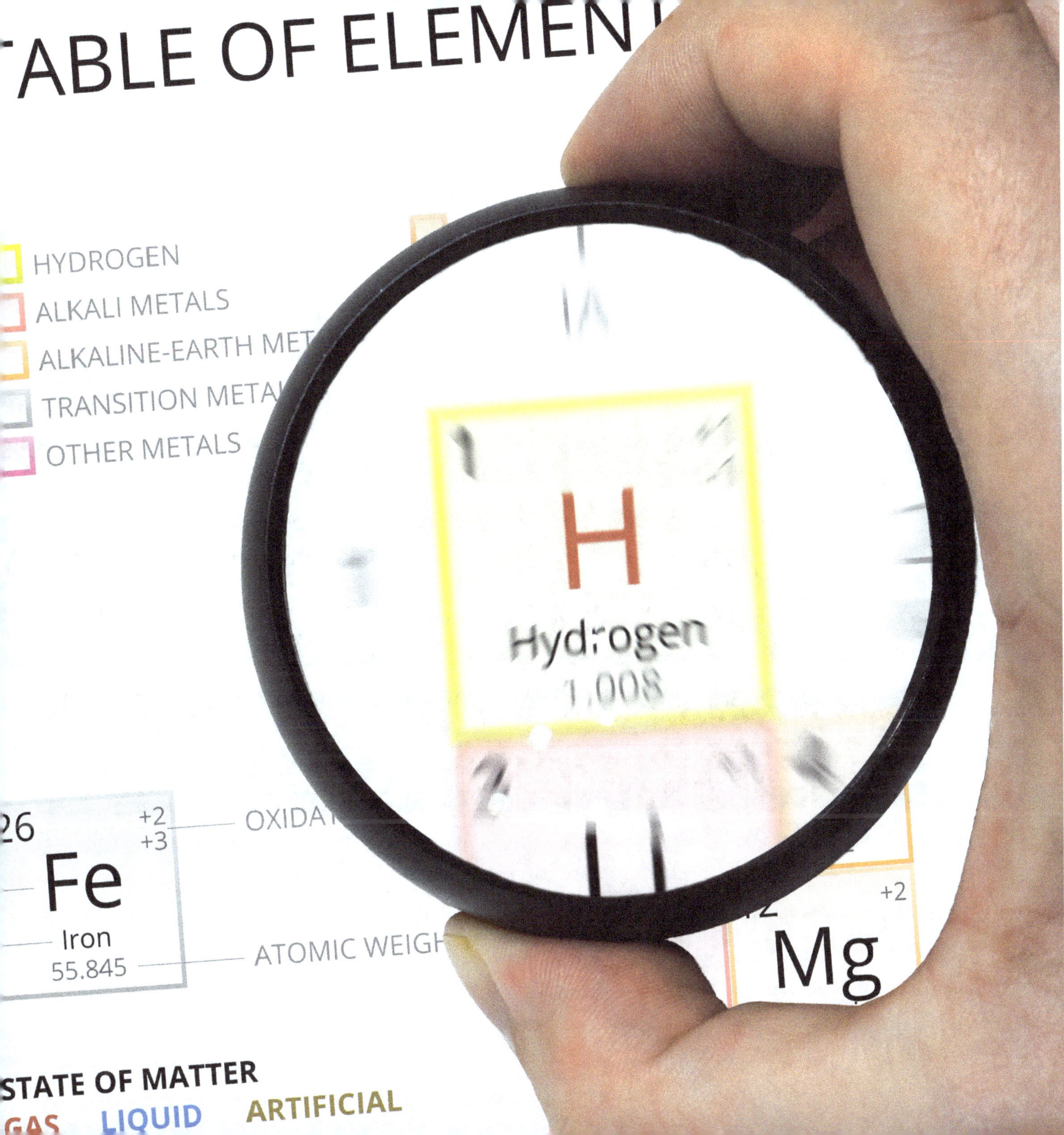
TABLE OF ELEMENTS
HYDROGEN
ALKALI METALS
ALKALINE-EARTH METALS
TRANSITION METALS
OTHER METALS
H
Hydrogen
1.008
26
+2
+3
Fe
Iron
55.845
OXIDAT
ATOMIC WEIGH
Mg
STATE OF MATTER
GAS
LIQUID
ARTIFICIAL

# PERIODIC TABLE OF THE ELEMENTS

Non-metal
Alkali metal
Alkaline earth metal
Transition metal

Metal
Metalloid
Halogen

Noble gas
Lanthanide
Actinide

The table is divided into groups in order to assist chemists working with these elements to learn and predict how an element may behave or react in certain situations.

This table lists the name and abbreviation for each element. You may find some abbreviations easy to remember, such as H which is the abbreviation for hydrogen but some like iron (Fe) and gold (Au) are a somewhat more difficult to remember. In the instance of gold, "Au" originates from "aurum", which is the Latin word for gold.

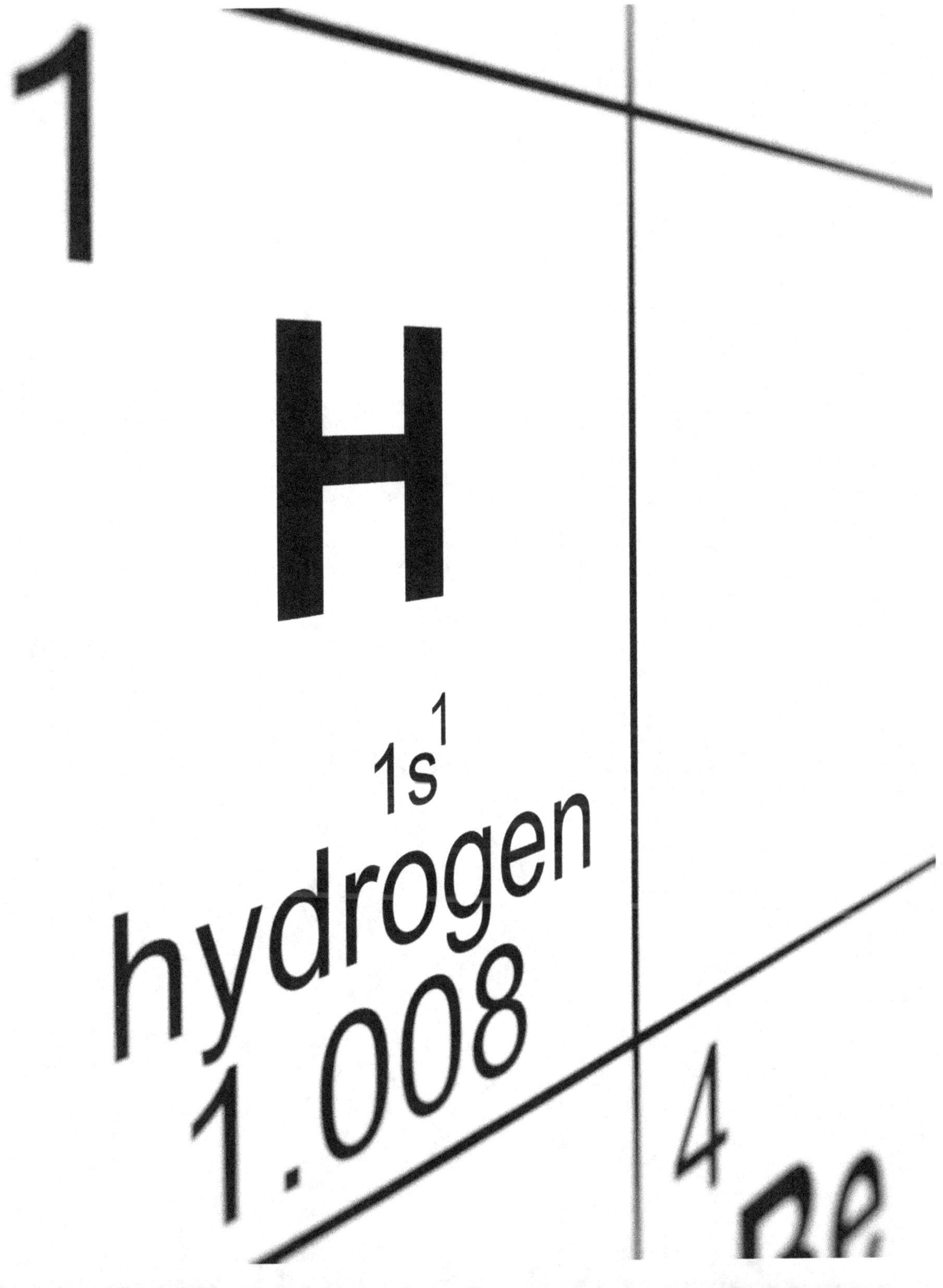

1

H

$1s^1$

hydrogen

1.008

4

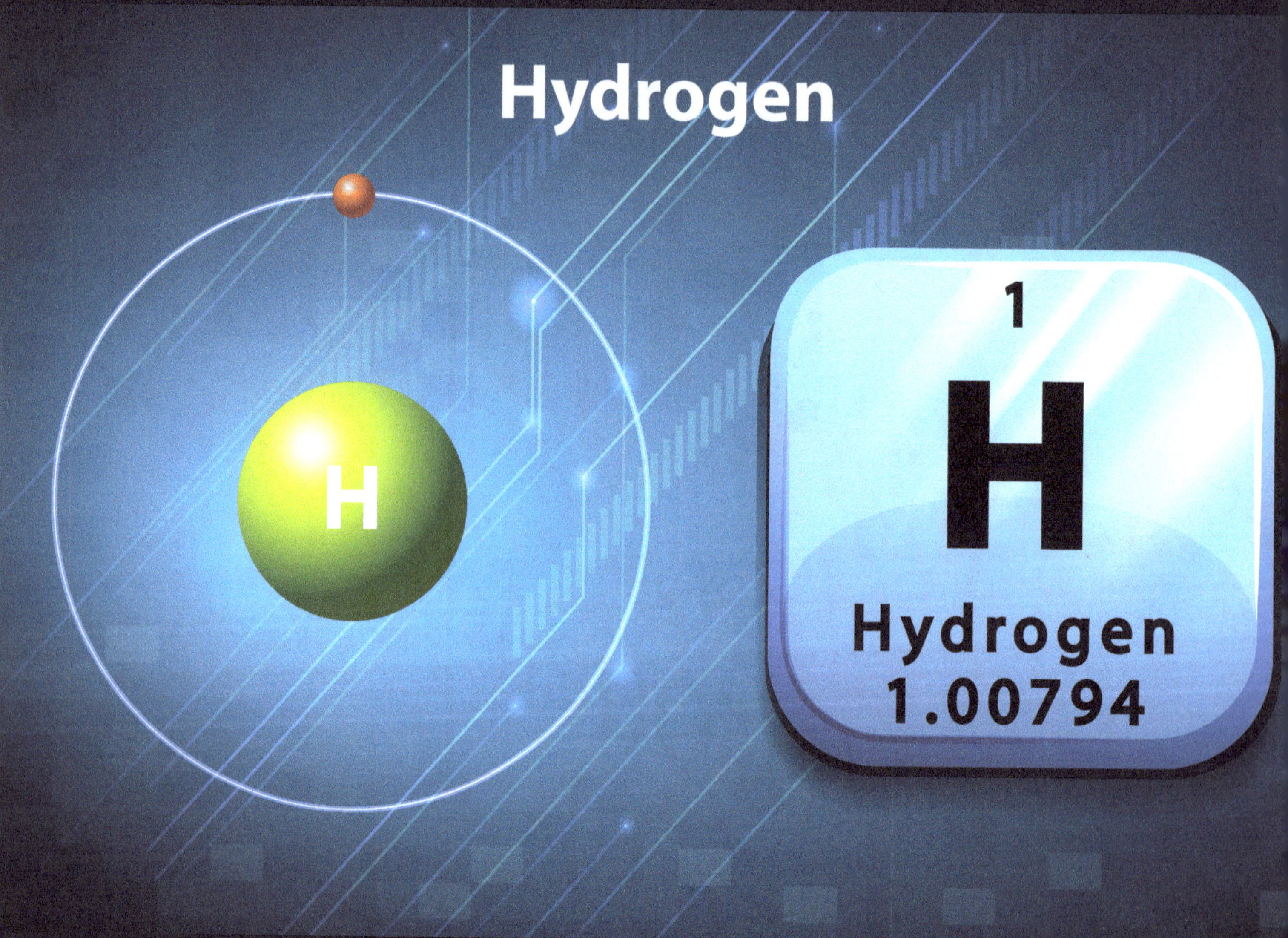

Hydrogen
H
1
H
Hydrogen
1.00794

You can learn more by researching on the internet or by reaching out to your teachers, parents, and friends for additional information. You will also find many experiments you will be able to perform with the guidance of an adult.

Visit
BABY PROFESSOR
EDUCATION KIDS
www.BabyProfessorBooks.com
to download Free Baby Professor eBooks
and view our catalog of new and exciting
Children's Books